As Seen Through Staggered Eyes

Séamus Fox

For Catherine

Enjoy!

Séamus

"...flesh, bone there is nothing there..."
Sylvia Plath

As Seen Through Staggered Eyes

A book of poems by
Séamus Fox

With editing by
Marcus Keeley

WILD WIND BOOKS
BELFAST

ISBN: 978-0-9560330-2-4

Published 2010 by

Wild Wind Books
Ormeau Business Park,
8, Cromac Avenue
Belfast BT7 2JA
Northern Ireland

info@wildwindbooks.com
www.wildwindbooks.com

For Steph

CONTENTS

Smiling

For Steph

I think of you every day
and you're always smiling.
You had no need of smiles
towards that end of yours.
It was so ungracious, like
you wanted us to know how
catastrophic existence can be.
I have stopped saying sorry
to the picture of you I have.
In the photo, you are smiling.
I couldn't look in your coffin.
They all told me I should look,
I am glad now I didn't,
and even though it nearly killed me
I am glad this is the way I remember.

Awake

The feelings never passed and other
people couldn't help themselves so
they aspired to be the saviours' of humanity.
Even the most selfish among them were only
disguising themselves that way while they
worried about all that was outside their control.
Assured egos will always need to ensure a form
of self preservation, not so at all though, they
were where we are at the clock that never ticks
because someone else is always tocking.
We laugh when we should be learning while
excusing ourselves via emotional treats and
with this very declaration I hypocritically
became an abstract apparition of myself.
There are so many things I should be doing
right now and sleeping is only one of them.

Into The Wild

For Christopher McCandless

You brave bastard,
you inspirational flutter
of humanity that seeps
and steals all my wishes.
I want to be you living on
that bus but I have an inability
to drive anything in this twenty
first century rut I dwell within.

I wouldn't endure a day out there,
even in an Alaskan summer
I wouldn't know how to catch
dinner or gather edible foliage.

You didn't just want to read
Tolstoy, Thoreau and London
you had to live the literature
instead of mere reader voyeurism.
A legend of solitude you stood
with nature and coursed a dream
of prehistoric proportions your
contempt for modernism, absolute.

Bored In The Pub?

I was asked by a man,
"Are you that bored?".
He was talking about
me writing in the pub.
Then he walked away
with his cue and a smile.
I stayed waiting for
a way to describe what
had just happened and
I thought for a moment
about how boring he
was being over there,
hitting insignificant balls
into holes in a table.

Perfect Circles

For Dean Fox

We all went camping and
I'd sit with my nephews,
Glenn and Dean, as they
would be drawing pictures.
Dean was about two at the
time and I have striking
memories of that day.
I was watching the boys draw and
our Deano started making
these perfect circles, they
were not part of a picture.
I looked at them and wondered
where he had hidden the penny.
I asked him to do it again and
he did, and again, another one,
he created about eight in a row.
Lots of other things happened but
I only remember the perfect circles.

Ancient Accident

I was among the men who
were building the gods, Mer.
I was completely feeble and
yet so strong when combined
with the mighty millions who
heaved the perfect cubed stones
to mimic the great belt of Orion.
Two ropes snapped and a one
tonne boulder pinned me to the
ground from the knees down.
I could not scream because
I knew I was now surplus as
my head was pulled up by the hair
and a short sword crossed off my
neck, flickering eyes, seven seconds
of energy left to deliberately drain.
I had no need of my remains as
sky to me back to feast on stars.

Why Do I Do This?

For Mum

Why do I do this ?
Why do I put myself through this ?
I am standing in the kitchen
trying to calm myself down
a wave of shame flashes over me
I've just been disrespecting my mother
sharpening my bitter caustic
tongue in her presence.
She's in her room now
I can feel her sadness lingering and
I am responsible for worsening it.
Why do I react that way? I know why,
many reasons, but explaining it would
be both useless and disturbing.
She's been looking for answers
ever since my sister died she's old
and has been grieving for a decade,
I feel fucking terrible.
I go in with my arms out and say sorry.
I wish I didn't have to say sorry,
I wish I knew what a peaceful mind was.
Why do I do this ? I know why and so does Mum.

The Light Darkness

Sometimes the darkness was
light, as in, not heavy and I
was even able to smile and
act like there was no death.
It was terribly confusing that
constant going back and then
being calm again, then back
and I could tell it was confusing
for others as well.
They looked at me oddly
and wondered why
I wasn't dribbling or stuttering.
I was gradually coping and had
gotten used to the changes in
mood, so when I would get those
feelings back I would avoid
people and wait until I was tranquil
before making little social attempts.
The ones who gave a fuck understood,
they left me alone and waited until
I was able to gather the strength to
go out and look at the world again.

A Decision To Make

You're thousands of feet up
in one of the world's tallest
buildings and a plane has just
struck it below where you are,
blocking off any escape routes.
The building then begins filling
with toxic smoke and the fires
begin moving toward your position
so you break a window not realising
it will further intensify the flames.
Now you're dangling out this window
and the flames are still advancing, the
heat is becoming too much to endure
as you take deep breaths of the cool
air outside and jostle with your
former colleagues for a place there,
away from the fire and smoke inside.
After about an hour or so of this
you can't stay there anymore; the heat
is now burning your skin and there is
only one thing you can do in order to
prevent that from happening.
You have a decision to make,
it's as simple as that.

Pomegranates

For Clare Mc Williams

She had pomegranates, so
strange-looking with their
red and yellow tones and
vulva-like openings and
hundreds of seeds that we
couldn't see but knew about.
We had nothing better to do
and we tended to talk at
length about the slightest
thing anyway, so we sat
discussing the pomegranates
trying to describe how weird
they appeared,
"They're like apples,"
I told her, "apples on acid."
She got the dictionary
and looked up "pomegranate"
then as she read the literal
description, both apples and
acid were mentioned "You see,"
I repeated, "apples on acid."

Relearning Curve

We are relearning
old knowledge -
all our energy is wasted
on trying to experience
what we already know.
Knowing how to make
love is not making love.
The act itself opens the
mind and gives sensations
that cannot be known
from the theory alone.
We do not simply want
to know how we want the
event to tingle on our souls.
We want to be left with an
impression in our memories.
All in life is a drug;
sunsets, love, moonlight, dancing,
melodies, words, eyes.
Everything shakes our feelings,
and when we wake at dawn
we will have changed again.

The Blackened Heart Of Love

I am black of mouth, cold to this heart
and dead in these eyes but I love you.
I am thin in this skin and Jurassic with depression
so gaunt and caught up with the legions of
the night but I am serious I still love you.

I have not forgotten much despite the way I look
disappointing days have become regularity now
that's why my kisses are gone but I swear
if I could I would love you.
I know the nights have folded your heart and
you have nothing left but a little kindness for
my listless arms but I love you and I loved you.

There is not enough tomorrow and while it may
have been all pretend I still seen a constellation
in your eyes and felt your hesitant compassion you
cannot hold my heart but from a distance I still love you.

I am fraught with danger and after myself quite
often looking at the humbling stars mostly.
I am as pale as those moonbeams the ones you
see when stars die while you fondle the depths of
more pleasing personalities, I am beginning to
doubt the existence of love but I love you, love you, love.

The Night Sky Road

I walk homeward in a frozen
night suffering with shivery
shudders as I search in my
empty pockets for a little heat
I may have left there earlier.

My mouth is emitting clouds
of precipitating mist, my pulse
is elevated somewhat as my
blood works to keep my iced
skin supplied with inner warmth.
The road is a mirror of hardened
glaciating glistening ice sheets
gradually joining like flat snowflakes
unfettered by the moisture that
remains in mud on steep banks
and occasional pot hole puddles.

I look up into the night with its
clear sky and the twinkles from
light years away and it's like the
night is looking down onto the
road and peering at its reflection,
sparkling there on the tarmac black.

A Lump Of Dope

For Mum

My mother shouted from
her room for me to be quick
and go out the back to get her
dope, a request which I thought
was confusing and funny.
I got up and went to see what
she was on about with a smile
across my slightly folded face.
"What did you say?" I asked her.
"Go out the back and get my lump
of dope will you before the dog
eats it", she said with a slight panic
from her usually tranquil voice.
"What's your lump of dope doing
out the back?" I asked.
"I was giving the dog biscuits out the window
and my dope was in the same pocket I had
the biscuits in so I dropped it
out by accident," she said
"Hurry out and get it before the dog
eats it, he'll be in an awful state."

Looking For Something

We always fight, love,
drink and dry, annoy,
insist, talk and enjoy
the selfish attention.

We murder and write
build and die, grow,
cry, effect and stare
into hypothetical days.

We trust and pander
hate and hold, paint,
fuck, touch and help
ourselves to hearts.

When doing nothing
we stand around in
our eyes looking at
all the other corpses
wondering where it is.

I've Been Called Worse

They poke me mentally,
call me Freud and giggle
with their backs turned.
All I do to attract these
reactions is try resolutely
to understand my condition.
I talk openly on humanity
because of a need to explain
our jumbled mentality and
complicated social structure.
I rarely make any assumptions
now and approach the actions
of others with an informed
set of questions that may help
me to arrive at reasoning.
The ones who have all the laughter
are not out to attain knowledge,
for if I were to judge them by
their actions they have no need
of it, as they seem to already know
so much about absolutely everything.

In The Shop

For May

I came out of the weather my
hood still up, and was greeted
by a behind-the-counter smile.
"Some weather out there" she said.
"Aye I know it's wild." I answered.
She began getting what I was
asking for: cigarettes, snickers, that
sort of thing; but she was hobbling
as she worked. "I hurt my back,"
she began telling me, "I was lifting a gas bottle."
"Not good," I said. "Once your back goes you're
done."She was giving me my change when
a man came quickly in to leave a
delivery then he was gone again.
"He hurt his back as well," she pointed
as the man hurried out into the rain,
"He was lifting jars of sweets."
"Jars of fucking sweets," I laughed
"Well at least you hurt yourself
on something half decent."
"Aye," she exclaimed with a
sigh, a tut then skyward eyes,
"and him a man and all."

Where Are You Working?

I know this man - no names
necessary - he's a good lad
but has become famous in
circles we mix in as being
one for coming out with
daft comments that embarrass
him and leave everyone in laughter.
He goes to get his haircut this
day with a friend of his who it
was that told me this story.
We have a local question here
it's the equivalent of talking
about the weather and it's always
asked during moments of silence:
"Are you working?"
So he happens to know the girl
who's cutting his hair and she
asks him where he's working.
He tells her where and all the
usual talk, how long he's been
there, crap pay, general banter.
Then he looks at her in the mirror
and says "Where are you working?"

A Half Pint Of Nothing

For Stacey Fox

"A half pint glass
of nothing", that's
what my niece
wanted from the bar.
As the barmaid
left I laughed at
her statement and
went to get my pen.
I was streaming with
my eyes and looking
for words with my
mind. A half pint of
Budweiser came back
with a confused person
holding it, and as we
kept laughing she looked
embarrassed until she
heard about the half
pint of nothing.

Guitar Girl

For Emer O'Neil

Our conversation consisted
of realisations and a brutal
understanding about the
unbridled nature of creative
and inwardly-facing glances.
Occasionally she actually looked
up at me and more than once
she said, "I am still listening."
She was still listening despite
the chords and the strumming.
I admired the fact that she was
not looking at me, for the very
creativity that was making her
hands into the music I heard
was the same beast that drove
me palpably into papered pens.
She was terribly committed as
was I and though our commitment
was different it was still commitment.

The Dark Empty Room

For Mum

I walked past the dark empty
room and the house was cold.
It felt unnatural, I was uneasy.
She was in hospital, that woman
who had given me all these breaths,
she gave me all my poems and
she made my star-straddled eyes.
I felt lonely even though we sat in
different rooms most of the time.
She was always there and now, not.
I put her room light on how she liked,
turned on her TV and drew the curtains
and when I sat down to write, I could
hear her television and part of me
thought she was there and felt calm.

Another Energy Poem

We are acting out our minds,
being the physical form of
all our staggered instincts.
Twisting hearts in our fingers,
injuring the days of others
with our loud dry mouths
filled with projectile phrases.
Some of us appear to have more
control or a more graceful way
of carrying out their days, while
others stutter in an awkward
interrupted flow causing waves
to ripple and fray into the calm.
From positive / negative minds
all the energy has nowhere to
go, so it just comes out through
hands that form many shapes,
friendly flat offerings or other
more violent cubes of bone.
Feelings seem never to end, they
leave us forever between the arms
of others or at doorsteps where
forgetfulness has a terrible price.

Immigrant Incident

I wait to go home with my
pizza box and my cigarette
and this lovely woman walks
toward me smiling, she is
olive in appearance. She has all
colours of roses for a pound a
piece and I decline politely.
A drunk woman comes from the
tiles and she looks at her and
says, "Get the fuck out of my face."
I say to her, "Don't be like that." and
she tells me about three Turkish
men feeling her ass. I reminded her
that she is not a man and may not
even be from Turkey. She reminds
me that they are all the same. I find
looking at her very difficult, she has
lipstick smeared across her fear, so I
turn away my head. Then this smile
comes to me, this lovely smile from
before and the roses again, subtle, with
her strange clothing, she asks my open
pizza box for a piece and I nod toward
the pepperoni and she thanks me twice.

04:53

Outside the world is getting
light, it is nearly being a day
out there beyond the window
and the pissed in my mind.
I have no shiraz left and the
Guinness is gone as well. I beat
them both although it wasn't a
race, more of an occupation really.
So here I am stuck in passing time
waiting for something to happen
and it will happen, because it did
before and I have known it always
to be this way. I nearly looked at the
time just then because I was going
to tell you how long this poem took,
when in reality, this poem is not ready.

Scattering The Gulls

Inspired by Anna Russell

In primary school, wasted crust
and left over triangles of bread
were taken by the caretaker to
the football pitch and scattered
there each afternoon like rubbish.
Lough Neagh was only a matter
of miles from there so they would
come in a black-white and grey
cloud, the gulls, all beaks and
hunger crying at the sky and
flapping then landing on webs.
There they tore at the field of
lunch with their jerking bird
movements and territorial jousts.
Hundreds of avian voices, high
pitched air off sharpened tongues.
At home time I would sneak up
as close as I could, then run to
them with my arms outstretched,
my mouth opening into noise
and lift them into the air like a
sheet being shook or a Mexican
wave, and I would look into
the rising cloud of feathers and
smile at the way they had scattered.

James Brown Funeral Directors

For Decky

On the Lisburn Road in
Belfast there is the hippest
most happening funeral directors.
Rather than dealing with the abstract
reality that is death they instead treat
their patrons to an alternative everlasting
afterlife driven by the soulful, melodic
groove-strewn graveyard shuffle.
James Brown funeral directors putting
the "Get up, get on up!" into an otherwise
dull and depressingly dismal deviation
from life. Helping your relatives "stay
on the scene like some undead machines."

Geophagy

In Haiti there is a trade
in dirt, a particular type
of smooth yellow earth
is sold in markets then
taken and made into
cookies. After salt and
shortening have been
added, the cookies are
shaped and left in the
sun to harden before
being sold at market
for two or three pence.
The woman who makes
and sells the "dirt" also
feeds herself and her
seven children on it.
She says she knows
it's not good for them
but it's either eat dirt
or don't eat anything.

Self Distraction

I was making tomorrow
using pieces of today
and swathes of yesterday
some of the pieces didn't fit,
not realistically anyway, but
they were the only pieces
I had so I just had to make them.
There was nowhere to hide my
blame all the previous places had
been used up and it never stayed
hidden for very long it always
came back and made me accept it.
After a time I had gotten used
to the way it all was, it all seemed
so normal like it was meant
even the obstacles didn't look
out of place any more, they just
furnished the background and
waited for me to fall over them.

Spitting Out Stout

My shoulder was fresh meat,
a strange place to watch
the strangled stars stumble.
She knew my plight. When
she gave me her number
she told me of phoning her
friend saying I was a bit rough,
still I loved her soul
without an edge in sight.
Her father was an alcoholic.
I sympathised with a hiss
of each fresh can struck,
brought her to my alcoholic
sister's grave. Our families
hindered in innocence,
an incoherent madness, unheard.
We spoke of her concerns
about the amount I was drinking,
then our clothes came off
and during heat of hedonism,
she would suck the stout
and spit it in my mouth.

Cassandra Told Me Secrets

The fractures will find you
basking in those pupils at
the slowing of dying ages.
Are not you driven grey yet?
What is wrong with your arms?
Does your soul have an escape?
I lay down with Cassandra on a
bed of yesterday and during pillow
talk she told me staggering secrets,
reaching in deeply and giving me
a shocking gift to tell the people
about tomorrow, but the people were
all so caught up with the immediate.
I walked to the corner of a metaphorical
room and waited patiently for the
youngest death I could wish for.
Cassandra stayed with me though, my
only comfort, she kept cutting me off
the tree. I had a torturous job to do
but even if the world was without belief
she whispered that they would all understand
one day, but unfortunately for me that day
would occur long after my expiration.

Thumbnail Impression

Four or five of us calmed in
the kitchen as the house music
made feet thump the floor ten
yards away through a door, into a
hall, before reaching another door.
The kitchen surfaces were rife
with rubbish, partly finished cans
and bottles abandoned hurriedly
for a myriad of unknown reasons.
Some had since became ashtrays.
A brief discussion arose as to who
owned which can and as a conclusion
was quickly reached, I watched the
owner push his thumb in near the top
of his can to create an identification tag.
I stood watching him thinking "good idea,"
I mean, have you ever drank cigarette
flavoured beer?

Goodbye November

I am not sure I can put
all the blame in your
days November, but
when I recount the years
past you always stank,
and not just of dead leaves
or a relative who dwindled.

I am a man of visible faults.
I have played with life and
sometimes lost. We always
lose in the end, but why are
you always there when I fail
November, outside the doors
that slam on gaunt winter nights.

I didn't notice you at first, November,
I knew you were not kind but
just last night on the thirtieth of you
as I walked bleak, dead leaf paths,
I made successive calculations and
noted your consistent inconsideration
for all the things I grew to be fond with.
Goodbye November, you
foul collection of brindled nights.

After The Tsunami

Some months after the tsunami
we still went out at the weekends
and laughed. We still worked and
had our little pockets of comfort;
the movies, hot cooked dinners,
uncontaminated water and our
loved ones alive in our arms.
Our local pub set up a charity darts
match and all the money raised
would be in aid of the victims
and survivors of the tsunami.
A woman in our company asked
what we would be doing on the
coming weekend and we explained
about the darts match and its aim.
"That tsunami was months ago," She
said, "it's played out."

The Englishman

A foreign driver came into
the warehouse so I greeted
him and he returned my words.
"That's a nice morning," he added,
"much better than yesterday."
"Aye," I replied "it's not bad is it?"
That was all I ever knew of him,
those few words about the weather.
As he left I realised he had a
Northern English accent and I
wondered why I had noticed that,
as it hadn't made any difference to
our conversation or to the weather
and yet there was a difference, else I
would not have thought about where
he came from. I held no malice toward
him, nor he to I and still there was a
difference there in my mind somewhere.

Consensual Surprise

She was going to the shop,
or so she said, and I asked
would she get me tobacco
while I puffed a dust-laden
cigarette paper, the last
of the previous packet.
We were laying around
laughing and looking at
each others naked skin.
"If you get me tobacco,"
I told her cheekily, "I'll
give you a surprise when
you get back; a consensual
surprise." Twenty minutes
later I was getting dressed
and as I walked from the
bedroom I said, "You're not getting
your consensual surprise now."
"You already gave me it earlier."
she giggled.

Wireless

For Johnny Magee

This forklift driver I was
working with told me he
had heard something on the
wireless and I said,
"Where is this 'wireless'?"
He said "the one up at the other door,"
and I said, "that's not a wireless."
He said, "well we used to call
them that years ago,"
and I said, "you couldn't have called that
one anything years ago because
it hadn't been made."
He said "yeah, but we used to call radios
'The Wireless' "
and I said, "but radios
have wires so they're not wireless."
He said, "Fuck off Fox, ya bastard,"
and walked away in a huff.

Train Sets And Dirty Books

For Andre Farrell

In my mid teens I decked
the attic and made a room
a place of escape, a place
to place my adolescence.
You would call and we'd
go up there and after putting
the train on repeat we'd sit
and look at dirty magazines,
but they were not dirty at all,
the women were very beautiful.
The train was only going round
its track to give an illusion of
sound down into the house so
my mother would think innocence
about our intentions for being there,
as our eyes went from picture to
picture, transfixed by femininity.
I thought I had the whole thing
secretive, thought mum never
knew, but she had raised men before
and one day she stood under the gap
in the ceiling and shouted up to us,
"I know what you two are doing up there."

Unpleasant Surprise

The can had punctured not
far from its apex and I really
should have noticed by its
lack of hiss on opening, but
having become soused by
the oodles earlier, I didn't.
I was laughing, holding it,
smoking a made up cigarette,
talking across the table
then I wiped at my eyes,
folded out my lips to meet
the metal and tilting back I
took a long, breathtaking gulp.
It was too late when I noticed
it was already past the back of
my throat. I spluttered a little,
wretched and held my
mouth then it was gone, that
dusty crusted blue/green float.
I looked at the can with its
millimetres of scarred metal
and pushed its hollow form
in and out in disbelief. Then I
didn't drink any more. Not from
that one anyway.

The Cans

The cans are falling
out of the bin. That
means there are too
many of them in there.

The contents of each can
ended up in my head
then ultimately, the earth.
Its only a small bin,

but I drank all those cans.
That means I am drinking
too much. I should do
something about it.

I'll empty the bin.

Strangely Shaded Moon

The moon looked imaginary,
bleeding discolouration,
it had a yellowish shade
across its enlarged face
and even its usually
darkish grey dry seas had a
a sepia like tinge to them.
It looked much closer and
heavier than on recent nights.
A gravitational masterpiece
draped there in the Christmas
eve darkness, behind the much
closer atmospheric mist that
was slightly scattered but still,
in the tranquil frozen last days
of an old and dying year.

A Cliché About Salt

"I am taking this with a
cliché about salt." I told
her, except I used the cliché.
She thanked me for that,
but in a sarcastic manner.
It was a dying phone call,
a very rhetorical phone call.
She knew and I knew and
I should have known from
the shape of my actions
that she knew all along.
I had known all along
looking back now, but her
way made me stay a little
bit longer. I cannot own
happiness, so I have to accept
what is offered to me and
hope I can just hold it for as
long as the laughter allows.

Rubik's Cube

For Lee Wharton

Half time in the match
gave us both a boredom
so extreme that you got
the Rubik's cube out.
"Bet you can't," I remarked,
"before the second half restarts."
That was enough for you,
your mind bent that plastic
into such colourful shapes.
In under three minutes there
it was, so squared and every
side so nearly the same.
"Bet you can't do it again",
I taunted you into another turn.
"Go then, mix it up for me."
you said. I ruined it for you,
messed up its whole sync
put it all so off colour,
and with minutes to spare
it was once again there;
a strange plastic thing
with very similar sides.

Avalanche Eyes

I fall down her then
get back up and fall
down her all over again,
as she makes her clothes
untidy piles on the floor.
I am stationary watching
her undress and get into
bed. I've not touched her
yet sensually, not today.
I just let my avalanche eyes
cascade down her length,
anticipating with patience.
I begin throwing my own
clothes into cognitive creases
but my eyes don't stop falling,
they keep making tracks up
and down her sedulous skin.
When I am ready to touch
her I begin falling all over,
but this time with my hands
and my lips. I keep open
my avalanche eyes to feel all
the magic that is woman.

Block

A few hours of relative
calm then my hand was
back to making pen shapes.

A Blind Bit Of Difference

Behind me when I sit at
my computer there is a
window without curtain,
and on brighter days the
suns reflecting upsets my
view of the screen and makes
me have to move into strange
positions to view the monitor.
My sister was saying she had
given my mother a reed blind
which was unused, and my
nephew went to get it to measure
it up to the rectangular window.
It fitted perfectly but when I
looked at the screen, the light
was still there, just slightly split
up into shining straight lines.
"It fits perfectly" my sister said
"Yes, but look," I said pointing at
the virtually unchanged reflection
"it doesn't make a blind bit of difference."

Cocaine Trampoline

I had a five pound note
stuck up my nose and the
powder-made euphoria,
a false euphoria but it was
nice to have that feeling at
my head, that gradual feeling.
As soon as it began I left the
house and out into the garden
and then up into the sky, up
and down with the cool night
getting earlier and the past
becoming some forgotten figment.
Bouncing, bouncing,
higher, higher.

A Stranger

I loved a stranger once,
she looked like all I needed.
She fell with me as all of life
stood still at a touch of lips.
My best friend, my lover,
I craved her when she was lost,
swam in the space left by
missing her inspiring aspects.
The seconds fell from us
like the happiest tenderness
tearing thin air with laughter
tucking us into the comfort.
The months folded up years
and her skin was always
until I touched another
softness and died in her days.
Occasionally I see a stranger
she looks familiar during small
talk and I keep peeping over
her shoulder avoiding her eyes
looking for someone I touched once,

but no one is never standing there.

The Drugs Are Working Fine

I take my first hit as she
enters my mind, in vision
alone and I read her skin,
already the drugs are beginning
to make light of my mind.
She falls closer and during a
sly smile her eyes drop then
rise to mine again at the very
same moment that she flushes a
cascade of hair over her shoulder,
nips her lip in her top row of teeth
and I take the inside of her fingers,
pandering into my palm and I use my
thumb to calm the skin above her knuckles.
I am giggling with tranquillity as
she presses her front unto mine and
now the pheromones and perfume begin
to further stupefy my mercurial mind.
Then with arms around my neck and the
deftest of tilts of her beautiful head she
offers me her left shoulder, slender,
as I take the first few lumps of skin
between my loose, longing lips
I realise testosterone is the only drug I am ever
going to need and it's working just perfectly.

Letting In Some Air

The music drills loud in the
background and the kitchen
table is a non-navigational
mass of bottles and cans and
ashtrays and scattered spillages.
A non-smoker sits opposite me
and I ask if he's okay; he looks
tired, he is squinting and his
eyes are beginning to look as
though a wasp has just left them.
Someone else also notices and
after making a slight opening in
the back door, he ushers the
non-smoker over for the freshness
in the cool post midnight air.
The puffy eyed patron then voices
his concern over the dog outside
as he makes his way to the gently
shifting wind-assisted blinds.
At this point the smoker begins laughing
while holding out his forefinger and
thumb as a comparison to the gap in
the patio door, "How's a fucking Rottweiler
supposed to get through there?" he
says, "it's not a fucking snake."

Stolen Sky

I stole the sky, wisped it
away into my memories
but I was unable to shake
it. It was too far from my
eyes and much, now, too
like my clouded mind.
I still have that memory
that I stole from the sky on
the calm, nearly sunny day
with the questionable breeze.
Sometimes I still look at it
with the other sky memories,
they are from days, nights,
all seasons. Faces can
be etched there, familiar faces,
strangers and occasionally
I will be there. I don't remember
ever being in a cloud but I was
once in a strange memory I have.

Horny As Fuck

I was waiting for something
to happen, something exciting.
We had been watching a documentary.
I really like documentaries but I
was in the mood for excitement.
I had my hand in my pocket, even
though there was nothing in there
except the lining that makes the pocket.
I could feel the excitement bulging
as she made her way down the stairs.
She came in having showered with
just a towel on and she smiled at me,
"I am horny as fuck" she said.
I stood up and took my hand from
my pocket just as she turned off the TV.

Woolloomooloo

For Clare Mc Williams

She offered me some wine
and after checking the label
I could only exclaim:
"what the fuck's it called?"
"Woolloomooloo" she
said quickly, as I tried to get
my head and tongue around
this very perplexing word.
"Wool-loo-moo-loo" I said,
slowly at first before gradually
getting faster as I became more
familiar with its litany of double Os.
"Woolloomooloo," I said confidently,
"that's a great word."
"I know,"she told me,
"that's why I bought it."

Near Impact

I felt a grimace closing,
my insides began folding
as my thoughts became
erratic and self explanatory.
My hand was changing in
my mind, I was thinking
about it becoming this skin
and knuckle box, all taught
and wanting some impact.
I was fostering anger, nearly
urging it to rise in my pupils
as streaks of evil flashed in
my overloaded oblong skull.
I began thinking "why?"
What good would be harvested
from striking this other person?
My muscles began to fall away,
tension leaving my fingers as
clarity began clearing a once
fraught space in my openness.
I took the fewest of steps to
an opening, then out and fresh
air, the sky and a deep breath.

Laser Guided

Pilots have no point of
reference to real sights
or feelings, they don't see
the faces of their victims.
They simply see the videogame
like images on the screen
then they point and click
and something explodes at
a nice, safe emotional distance.
There are times when humans
make mistakes and pilots are
human, so when episodes of
friendly fire occur they do have
to see their victim's faces and
hear names and watch families
disintegrating
and eat themselves from the inside out,
and in the back of their minds is that screen
which replays that laser guided moment,
forever.

White Lines

For Neal Crangle

We were in the warehouse,
supposed to be working,
but we were talking instead
about some subject that won't
change this poems direction
drastically and that I have forgot.
Over in a corner a radio was
blaring it was tuned to
Radio Two. Suddenly 'White Lines'
by Grandmaster Flash and
the Furious Five starts playing.
With those jumbled sighs at
beginning and both of us just
looked at each other in amazement.
"Holy Fuck," I exclaimed,
"you know you're getting old when
Radio Two starts playing shit you like."

Backwash

For Bernie and Kirsty Cahoon

There was very little milk left
and we were in the process of
making tea when she decided
to start sipping from the carton.
She already had a mouthful by
the time her mother realised and
went to snatch the carton from her
"Fuck's sake there's not much left."
She just laughed and said "You can
have it then and I hope you
both enjoy the backwash."
There was just enough milk for
two cups of tea and as we sat at
the table and sipped I asked
"Does your tea taste funny?"

Love Is Only A Word

'Love' is only a word,
a description, a lie.
It is not a kiss or that
beauty you fucked once,
or the way your stomach
used to go when her eyes
took delight from the stars.
Language is too simple to
describe the mutilation of
a heart by a less than
careful selfish hand that
just moved off too find
another carefree emotion.
'Love' is only a word as are
'hate' and 'fuck' and 'death'.
'Love' may as well be
'hate' and 'fuck' and 'death'
sometimes it feels that way.

Keep It Simple

For Dessie

The man sat swaying at
the bar, a small pile of
euro notes and coins in
front of him so the barman
didn't have to wait for his
his incoherent head to count.
He looked at me nodding
slightly without meaning it and
said, “have you got it figured out?"
I said, “no", even though I was
unsure what exactly it was that
I may or may not have figured.
Then he said “Keep it simple."
I sipped my stout and thought
about it and I came to the conclusion
that had I drank as much as he had
I would definitely be keeping it simple.

Smile For Daddy

For Jeff and Ebony

I watched him with my
eyes making water, it
was a stunning thing
to watch my niece had
given him this little
reddened hours old
package of humanity.
I had never seen him
smile so much but it
was not a normal smile,
it was coming from inside
every sinew he possessed,
it looked like this was it
the reason for living, the
meaning of all life, the very
essence of our existence.
I felt pleasure to be able to
see it happening, he lay her
Lilliputian body on the bed
then put his face close to
hers and gently waving her
miniature hand he said
"Smile for Daddy."

Number One Syndrome

When someone goes wrong
we just nuzzle into the next
available heart with new purrs
and sighs to content us for
another few moments of life.
If the car breaks we buy another,
the TV starts blinking we think
about a better more viewable one,
bins get emptied, movies always
end, water evaporates, life is dry.
We may as well be houses
with no back doors and hearths
that ring a cold lack of fire.
We have number one syndrome
and that's how wars are won.

A Random Beauty

She stood before me shining
stunningly and so womanly
her eyes were almost jade.
I had never seen such a colour
in the eyes of another human.
Her voice, her smile, softness
there upon her silk-kissed face,
slightly shy in public, yet demonic
when I placed my lust inside her.
I drew her to me and pressed her
at my already slivering skin.
I touched the goose bumps at
her neck and filled her lips
with the fullness of my love.
For only moments I touched
her then a cash register rang,
she handed me my change and
a receipt then I left the shop.

The Days And Nights

The days and nights
turned into each other
and twisted on like a
mass of bleeding hours,
awake and asleep and
all strangely relative.
I had lost my regard
for the ambling routine
so I found myself waking
at odd, unflinching hours,
drawing tranquility from the
times that others associated
with the shutting of eyes.
I wasn't carrying the days
with any degree of grace.
My journey was stuttered
and it slowed at times to a
near halt but I always seemed
to get back up and leave the
darkness. Just long enough to
fool myself and the others
into thinking something had changed.

A Lack Of Thought

When you have your back
to them they are making a
semi-fictional person from
your life and not once thinking
twice about their discretion.
They have deafness with those
broken smiles they display and
bloodied incandescent white
that rolls up into their eyelids.
Their knowledge lasts a moment
and cannot wait until tomorrow
for it all must happen now, it all
must be understood no matter
what means need be disposed.
When nothing has been changed
and no objective has been reached,
they look the other way and find
some other opportunity that has
equally as little thought and
ultimately the same consequence.

Chemicals And Poetry

I kept breaking on and off.
I loved life but it had become
increasingly difficult to look at.
Dependence on chemicals didn't
help nor did the loneliness but
said dependence had caused the
loneliness, and now it was helping
to defeat having no woman to love
but only until the hangover came.
I was always uneasy, wanted stimulation
mental, physical, anything just to take
myself out of the jumbled thoughts
that were ransacking everything that
made my eyes even slightly glow.
I was pouring poetry into the void,
it was often dismal because the likes
of Plath and Bukowski may have been
wonderful wordsmiths, but they mirrored
my excessive edge. Maybe that was
part of the reason why it continued.

Collective Judgment

We do not see the world
through the eyes of an
individual, we often listen
to the others and foster
their views, maybe because
we hold them in regard or
because we have difficulty
thinking for ourselves.
Judging is something we
do in groups, rather than
knowing a person personally.
We save our efforts by simply
listening to the local talk.
The stories become more
exaggerated with each mouth
that joins the verbal lynch mob
and when we talk to the person
we avoid their eyes because
we know things about them that
they have never even done or said.

Socially Inept

We like other people's business
and want to know what they're
up to, that's why soap operas
are popular, we are all voyeurs.

We whisper in closed gatherings
nodding for more confidence,
accepting just for the comfort
denial becoming an art form.

We talk and gasp at the stories
about other people while they
talk and gasp at stories about us,
not many look at themselves and

those who do are considered inept.

The Single Bed

For Lee

The single bed
was uncomfortable
physically, but from
an emotional angle
I loved it's closeness.
We were getting to know
each other's skin. I was
musing about the constellation
I had discovered in her eyes
as I stroked her face.
When she took my left
arm and began exploring
the sadness of my scars.
She made a line between
arteries with her finger
and told me that her
mother had made a fatal
incision in that place.
I told her I was sorry,
then we forgot about
death and made love again.

All The Same

I see things different,
it doesn't mean I am
better than other people,
could even be worse.

If I am different than them,
they're not the same as me,
meaning everybody is different
and that makes us all the same.

Two Couches

There were two couches separated
making a splayed L shape and
drooling candles everywhere,
burning themselves hurriedly out.

We had been crazy with lust for
two long hours or more and now
calmly sat near-naked on a couch each,
reading poems to each other
and looking for universal answers.

We discussed the ways in which
we had caused each other to tingle
so sensationally and sensually,
rejuvenation and growth,
and how we came to be so
lustfully attentive and lengthy.

I should have went over to her
couch and held her, the candles
would have liked that, they'd
have shuffled slightly and I'd
have made her sigh again.

I think about this all the time but
thoughts are only made of the past,
and while memories are thoughts,
some of them make very needy nights.

My Literal Lover

For Sylvia Plath

I think I have fallen
for a dead poetess.
She is dark, fraught
with bleeding flowers,
Nazi symbolism,
bags full of god and
other equally striking
metaphors for heaven.
She was exquisite with
language drawing sighs
and laughter and tears
but it is not about her
story, which was tragic,
it is her way on the page
that blushes in my mind,
simple yet so complex.
She enthuses me with her
voice, she speaks through me
into the empty room.
Simply knowing her words is not
sufficient, I must hear them.
No living woman could give
what she has left me with.
Love in a literal sense is much,
much more fulfilling than all
that over rated pushing and
waiting for the phone to not.

Clock

I woke to just watch
the last moments of
a day slipping slowly
beyond the present - then.
There were three hands
playing out near tangible
time, clicking mechanically.
One's speed was so immediately
apparent, the seconds ticked
much less and the third appeared
not to move even slightly.
So I sat and watched that day
getting slowly away,
and there was such calm on the face of it.

The Psychology Of Self

It's always different; looks,
feels different, it even sounds
like there are no similarities,
but all those little differences
between the picture you have
of your self inside, and the way
you react with the world are
ambiguous because you will find
the state of your life to be a
direct reflection of a lot of what
happens at your fingers very tips.
I am not saying we should avoid
our emotions but occasionally we
should just step into the shade
and look at how similar we are in
comparison to the world we feel
so different from, we should drag
our egos down from that self-styled
pedestal we so carefully formed with
all of those beautiful intentions and
we should notice all the others who
smile upon the slightest glow of positive.